STORNOWAY PRIMARY SCHOOL
JAMIESON DRIVE
STORNOWAY

KT-161-857

Families are made of people who
love each other.
There are small families with
just two people.

2

And there are big families with lots of people of all ages!

Try this later
Draw a picture of your family.
What is it like?

Some families have lots of children.

And there are families where the children
have all grown up
and have families of their own!

In fact there are many different
kinds of families.
Sometimes the whole family
lives together.
There are lots of people to
help each other.

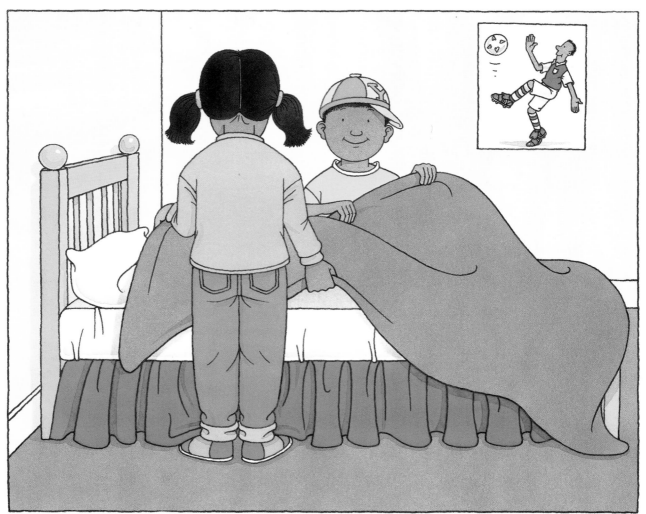

Now try this

How many people live with you in your family?

What kinds of jobs do you share?

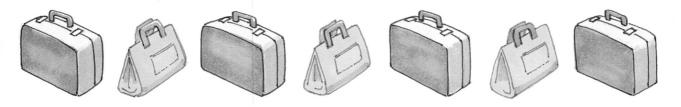

Sometimes people live separately.
They might come to visit at the weekend
or to stay for a holiday.

11

Some people have families far away in another country.
They cannot see each other very often but they can stay in touch.

Families share special times together.

Now try this
What is the name that you were given
when you were born?
What is your family name?
Who else shares your family name?

Families help each other through difficult times as well.

No one knows you as well
as your family does.

Now try this
Think of all the things you share with people at home.
Do you like the same things?
Do you look like each other?

Many families keep photographs of special occasions.
Some of them were taken a long time ago.

Try this later

Find a photograph that shows your family before you were born. Ask someone to tell you about the people in the photograph.

Your family began a long, long time ago.
Ask someone to tell you stories about
your family in the past.
Would you like to have a family of your
own one day?